Speckled Birds

by Shirley Lauro

A SAMUEL FRENCH ACTING EDITION

SAMUEL FRENCH

FOUNDED 1830

NEW YORK HOLLYWOOD LONDON TORONTO

SAMUELFRENCH.COM

ISBN 978-0-573-69800-2   Printed in U.S.A.   #29309

MUSIC USE NOTE

Licensees are solely responsible for obtaining formal written permission from copyright owners to use copyrighted music in the performance of this play and are strongly cautioned to do so. If no such permission is obtained by the licensee, then the licensee must use only original music that the licensee owns and controls. Licensees are solely responsible and liable for all music clearances and shall indemnify the copyright owners of the play and their licensing agent, Samuel French, Inc., against any costs, expenses, losses and liabilities arising from the use of music by licensees.

Music and lyrics for "Great Speckled Bird" and "Down in the Valley" are in the Public Domain.

IMPORTANT BILLING AND CREDIT
REQUIREMENTS

All producers of *SPECKLED BIRDS* *must* give credit to the Author of the Play in all programs distributed in connection with performances of the Play, and in all instances in which the title of the Play appears for the purposes of advertising, publicizing or otherwise exploiting the Play and/or a production. The name of the Author *must* appear on a separate line on which no other name appears, immediately following the title and *must* appear in size of type not less than fifty percent of the size of the title type.

SPECKLED BIRDS was first produced by Amie Brockway with the Open Eye Theater in Margaretville, New York on May 17, 2003. It was directed by Sharone Stacy. The cast was as follows:

ANGIE (EVANGELINE) . . . . .Alisa Fersch

THEO . . . . Max Sapinsky

GRANDMA. . . . . .Agnes Laub

CLARICE . . . . .Enda Nolan

DAD . . . . Richard DeGenero

MISS DUVAL . . . . Patricia Van Tassel

SPECKLED BIRDS was presented in part by grants from the A. Lindsay and Olive B. O'Conner Foundation.

CHARACTERS

ANGIE (EVANGELINE) – A country girl. Somewhat naïve. 14. Freshman in high school. Tall, lanky, athletic build but with long, lovely hair, a soulful, beautiful face and a courageous soul. She wears make-shift athletic, then too big jeans and shirt, with her shirt-tail hanging out and later, good athletic clothes. White *(see Author's Note)*.

THEO – A little older than Angie. Awkward, clumsy, ungainly in some way. Can be very tall, thin, or heavy. Teasing nicknames can be "TEDDY BEAR" or "TEDDY TWIG," etc., depending on his physical demeanor. Brilliant computer "nerd." Great heart and sense of humor but painfully shy and needy. White.

GRANDMA – 70ish. Strong featured, Appalachian woman descended from generations of coal miners. A woman who's come through hard times and survived. Likeable, wise, tough and strong as bespeaks her heritage – but aging now. White.

DAD – 30ish. His spirit appears in play as Angie remembers him when he went to War: a strong, warm hearted father and a genuine Appalachian man in a camouflage War uniform. White.

CLARICE – Late 30s. Wears what she thinks are extremely attractive clothes that show her off, although she's a little too plump, and they don't. Hostess of the Crystal Café, where she wears black short dress, frilly which apron, very high heels. Angie's aunt by marriage. Calls it as she sees it, but doesn't see it. Or calls it – because she is a kind of a "Knoxville Mrs. Malaprop" – misusing and mispronouncing words. But thinks her syntax and vocabulary're great. Clarice is also lonely and stuck in her life and needy of love. She is trying to overcome this. Somehow. White

MISS DUVAL – Middle-aged woman *(No male substitution, if possible)*. Suit, glasses. Projects a sweet, naïveté, coupled with a prissy, "I'm only here to help and I am right, good, wonderful" quality. Underneath, she wants to hang onto her job and turf above all, and is desperate that there be no cause trouble, scandal, or suspicion anywhere near her. White.

SETTING

A small, rural American town somewhere in the Appalachians. There is a sharp split in the community between the "haves-and-have-nots."

TIME

Now.

AUTHOR'S NOTES

Play is not realistic. Sense of fluidity throughout. An other-worldly quality to piece that should sift through the play beneath its surface.

It is possible that the character of Angie could be played by an actress of an ethnicity other than White.

*To Joshua, and the world of Angies
and Theos in which he lives.*

ACT I

(Lights up. A corner of high school stadium. A boy, **THEO** *sits on bleacher back to audience.)*

LOUDSPEAKER. *(V.O.)* ...And...the qualifying runners for the varsity girl's relay team are: number 19, Lindsay Saybrook; number 42, Jennifer Caldwell; number 11, Margaret Swift; number 90, Anna Jo Brooks; number 48, Liza Durand.

Report to Coach's office following completion of try-outs, please. Next category: girls' 50 yard dash. Entrants report to start line please. Entrants competing for places in the varsity 50 yard dash come to start line please: Sudie Peppercorn, number 57; Juliet Spooner, number 59; Elizabeth Shay, number 92; Angie Trueblood, number 53 –

*(***ANGIE*** appears, band around forearm marked "53." Large boys boxer shorts, large boy's T-shirt, old canvas sneakers.)*

Joleen Smith, number 12, Mary Lou Hunter, 56; Susannah Fairly, 7, Gwynda Johns –

*(As names drone on, ***ANGIE*** rips off armband. She moves down aisle and away from field as ***THEO****, the boy, rises, looking after her.)*

Numbers 57, 59, 92, 66, 56, 7, present. Number 53 absent. 53?? Angie Trublood??. Absent. Not accounted for. Report start line immediately 53!

*(***ANGIE*** pauses, looking back.)*

Start line. ANGIE TRUEBLOOD, 53. REPORT!

*(***ANGIE*** moves farther, faster away.)*

53?? 53??

(She discards armband.)

LOUDSPEAKER. *(cont.)* DISQUALIFIED!! Report to coaches office #53. Disqualified from try-out competition. ANGIE TRUEBLOOD! REPORT!

(THEO exits as ANGIE moves from area faster, running to new area: lights up. Old style aluminum trailer. Rickety rail porch attached catwalk ladder to roof. ANGIE looks around warily, skins up ladder to trailer roof, goes to old trunk, takes out athlete's trophies, guitar, militarily folded American flag, votive candles and matches. She puts statues, candles in circle, lights candles and sits in center clutching flag. Trailer door opens. CLARICE appears in waitress' hostess outfit, and hat.)

CLARICE. Angie?

ANGIE. *(startled)* Aunt Clarice?

CLARICE. Thought I heard you banging around up there. Get down!

(ANGIE blows out candles, comes to roof edge.)

ANGIE. But it's not first of the month.

CLARICE. I am not gonna bust my lung brayin like a mule! Get down!

(ANGIE starts down.)

Now, listen up! Right in the middle of my most important hostessing shift – at the Crystal Cafe – when all them tips of substantiation come rolling in? The clinic from *here* calls me to come up here from all the way down to *Knoxville! Immediately!* On account of what your Grandma did.

ANGIE. CLINIC?

(She skins hurriedly down the rest of the way.)

CLARICE. I'm the responsible relative they say and have to drive clear up here to her bring her home.

ANGIE. She's here?

(ANGIE starts into trailer.)

CLARICE. Asleep! And leave her be!

ANGIE. What happened?

CLARICE. Took the wrong medicine. Got dizzy 'n fell! Then she gets up – which she shouldn't have moved of course – calls 911 and ends up at the clinic. Where they locate me. You give out the phone number of the Crystal Cafe to that Miss Dimwit Duval Social Worker over there?

ANGIE. Grandma's all right?

(She makes a start again to trailer.)

CLARICE. Leave her be! Like I said she is sleepin it off. Could've chewed the whole bottle here alone of course Why she could've broke her neck with them bones of osteoporosis she's growin and that Brain State Predicament's that's about to settle in.

ANGIE. Last check-up the doctor said older people all have brittle bones.

CLARICE. *(studying* ANGIE*)* Angie?

ANGIE. What?

CLARICE. I am gonna tell you something, Angie – there is not a normal situation in her instance...

ANGIE. Huh?

CLARICE. At the clinic conference – where I just was – I have had privately confirmed by the doctor – there is an osteoporosis diagnosis for her. And a peculiar Brain State of Confusion settlin in.

ANGIE. It's not what he told me last month at her check-up.

CLARICE. *(still studying her)* Also – that Miss Dimwit Duval Social Worker? She stipulated – before she cut out – this not a fit place for her to live. Especially when I imparted how the heat here is on the bum.

*(*GRANDMA *appears in trailer door,* ANGIE *running to her. Embrace, and kiss.)*

ANGIE. Grandma, Grandma! You okay?

GRANDMA. Old Grandma's fine, sweetheart – but, look it here – what're you doin home so early?

ANGIE. They – they let out early – teachers' conference! Sure you're okay?

GRANDMA. Have to watch them pills is all.

CLARICE. Pill's is only the start of the trouble that's been borrowed here. How long you think before something else rears its ugly head and really cracks her neck? When she forgets and commits a more dangerous act on account of her Brain State? Clearly this situation has come to a rolling boil.

GRANDMA. Clarice, I'm gonna tell you something: Angie and me can solve whatever problems go on here.

CLARICE. Well, that was then and this is now. And where you are is what you've done!

GRANDMA. (glancing at twilight, suppressing a smile) Well, where we are is about night, Clarice. And we just know how you don't like to drive that truck of Brewster's on the highway nights.

CLARICE. Rattle trap that it is. And all that son of yours has managed to provide these many years. Includin *no steady job.*

GRANDMA. (chuckling softly) Well now, Brewster? Probably better if he'd've stayed country, Clarice.

CLARICE. (stunned) And miss the lights of Knoxville?

GRANDMA. Well –

(GRANDMA, chuckling, imitating Brewster: slow, lilting voice, ambling gait of a large, patient, man:)

We all know he's like his Daddy 'n his Daddy's Daddy 'n his Daddy's Daddy's Daddy! All of 'em sweet slow goin coal minin men.

(ANGIE laughs. CLARICE is not amused.)

CLARICE. Minin days is yesterday's mail. But "slow" sure hits him on the head!

(CLARICE starts off.)

GRANDMA. Take care now –

CLARICE. *(rambling to herself as she goes:)* Two of 'em livin like wack-a-doo gypsies – perched on the throughway – and who knows what comes roarin off that exit on their motorcycle with tattooed muscles and rings through their nose!

(She exits.)

*(**ANGIE** and **GRANDMA** burst out laughing.)*

ANGIE. She's a piece a work, Grandma – I don't like her much –

GRANDMA. *(still chuckling)* Don't pay her any mind, honey – Clarice is twenty minutes once a month to us, 25 dollars cash, and two pieces of her restaurant coconut pie.

(pause)

ANGIE. Maybe. I don't trust her. Wish they'd called *me* from the clinic instead.

GRANDMA. Told 'em not to on account of your try-outs. I –

(She looks at her.)

Lord, darlin, you make it to that varsity team? I forgot to ask…

(beat)

ANGIE. *(not looking at her)* Uh – um-hmm…I did…but I –

GRANDMA. *(interrupting, tremendously excited)* Prayed my heart out to God for it, Angie!

(She hugs her.)

Gonna get first, like your daddy: school athletic trophies – name called right out at them assemblies – before he went to War…

*(**ANGIE** looks at her, trying to tell her something:)*

ANGIE. Mmm – Grandma- I –

GRANDMA. *(interrupting, not hearing)* Now *you're* gonna make our dream come true! Win us some a them trophies! Get you one a them athletic scholarships to college. Be a coach or teacher sometime! Give Ole Grandma somethin to live for. Oh, Lord, let that Dream happen one day!

(From pocket of sweater on rocker, she pulls bill, gives it to **ANGIE**.*)*

GRANDMA. *(cont.)* Buy somethin pretty for your hair? Combs with them sparklies? A barrette? To celebrate what you done today.

*(***GRANDMA*** kisses* **ANGIE**, *puts sweater on.)*

Chill's in the air.

*(***GRANDMA*** goes in.* **ANGIE** *runs to roof, sobbing. Lights out, then up: shadowy corner of stainless steel and black marble kitchen. Counter, fridge, stool.* **THEO** *enters, flips on pendulum light that swings, throwing ominous shadows. Stainless steel fridge and black marble counter gleam. Laptop sits on counter. And birdcage with bird. He turns on laptop, talks to bird:)*

THEO. Time for dinner at the Mansion
Gated houses on the hill!
With birdseed for my Speckles.
So eat girl! Get your fill!

(He pours seed into trough, chuckling.)

My Speckles gets Hartz Mountain.
Poured as fast as Theo's able –

(Now puts frozen food from fridge in microwave.)

Then Theo zaps his Healthy Choice
One, two, three, four

(Microwave rings.)

And it's ready
For the table!

(He sits at counter with food.)

Hey, Speckles? "No T.S. Eliot, no Robert Frost, Huh? Huh? But not too bad for your Big Bleep Boss!"

(He laughs at this rhyme too.)

Huh, girl, huh? Pretty good rhymester, punster, Joke of all Trades?

(He laughs, remembers something:)

Oh! Speckles? The M&M's! I have forgot!

And we know how Theo needs a lot!!"

(He pulls two pound bag of candy from drawer, eating some. Computer bell sound then voice from laptop.)

VOICE. *(V.O)* You've got mail!

THEO. *(jumping from counter, ecstatic)* Hey, hey, hey! *THEO HAS MAIL?*

(He jams M&M's in mouth, punches key on computer, talking to it:)

'OPEN!'

(reading)

"Rik from Reykjavik!"

(to bird, ecstatic)

Oh God, Speckles? The teen from Iceland? Remember when Theo went on THE CHAT ROOM? Yesterday? Dinnertime, old girl? And found a message: "Rik of Reykjavik, high school sophomore, seeks same with American teen"? Remember I answered? Now *he's* answered me! From Iceland!

*(***THEO*** *reading laptop.)*

"What's up with you? Theo?"

*(***THEO*** *turns to Speckles.)*

"What's up with you? Theo?" He's rhyming! Speckles? He rhymes too!

(continues reading:)

"In answer to your question: Yes, it *is* midnight in Reykjavik when it's dinner time in the good old U.S.A. It's midnight now!"

(to Speckles)

Oh my God, Speckles? Night's turned to day, day's turned to night! He's taken the trouble to write *me* at midnight! Awesome to even *think* about, huh, old girl?

(reads more)

THEO. *(cont.)* "So who are you, Theo Green?"

(to Speckles:)

Oh Jesus Christ in heaven! He wants to know about Theo?

(typing, reading)

"This – is – Theo – and – this is – about – Theo – he has Speckles, his bird – and – in the yard he's got – five – cats – three dogs – from – Bide-a-wee–"
Send!

(Punches "Send" key. A beat, then computer bell sounds goes off, he clicks key. Reading:)

"What is Bide-a-wee"?

(laughing:)

Oh, that is very rich, isn't it, Speckles, old girl – that is very, very rich: he keeps on wanting to know!

*(**THEO** typing, reading:)*

"A – place for abandoned strays – the cats and dogs. Speckles was in yard with broken wing. Pushed from nest by others. THAT DRIVES THEO NUTS!"

(Punches "Send" key. A beat. Computer bell sounds. **THEO**, *reading:)*

"Who helps? Brother? Sister? Mom or Pop?"

*(**THEO** pauses, then types.)*

I nurture animals. Only child with so-called "Mom and Pop." "Dentists is the better name! They're never home."

(Clicks "Send" key. A beat. Computer bell sounds.)

THEO. *(cont.)* *(reading:)* "What the hell's nurture mean?

(typing, reading:)

Webster's Collegiate Dictionary – nurturer: "one – who supplies food – protection – and promotes growth."

(Clicks "Send" key. Beat. Computer bell sounds. **THEO** *Reading:)*

"Hello? Stray animals and words all you're into? You into Shaq? NFL? My favorites maybe: The Braves?

(**THEO** *wolfs down candy, starts typing.*)

"Not into sports – don't follow them – "

(*Punches "Send" key. Beat. Bell sounds.*)

(**THEO***'s stunned as scans message. Silence. Then, barely able to read:*)

"Sorry. Signing off – Peace out – "

(*Types, reads. Very desperate:*)

Peace – out – Rik –

(*Punches "send" key, turns off computer, gobbles candy bar from pocket, picks up the cage, starts pacing around with it, turning lights out, one after another.*)

So – well – Speckles – that was something, huh girl? Little interlude anyhow? But now what, old girl? Now what? Now what? Now what?

(*All lights out. Lights up on roof.* **ANGIE** *sitting, tightly clutches American flag. Guitar is beside her. She gets up, lights candles, sits in middle of the circle. She looks around slowly, as if expecting something.*)

ANGIE. Down in the valley
The valley so low.
Hang you head over –
Hear the wind blow.

(**ANGIE** *stops singing. Whispering:*)

Daddy? Our song? Hear it? I haven't called you for so long! But hear it now and come! Please come!

(*Looking around, then sings again, very softly:*)

Roses are red dear,
Violets are blue –
Angels in heaven,
Know I love you.

(*Now whispers softly:*)

ANGIE. *(cont.)* Please!

> *(She starts singing again:)*
>
> Roses are red dear,
>
> Violets are blue –
>
> *(In distance we hear* **DAD**'s *voice:)*

DAD. Angels in heaven
Know I love you…

> *(Now she sees him on roof in diffuse, surreal, whitish light. He wears a camouflage uniform, as he wore when He went to War. He always says what she remembers him saying when he was alive. And he relates to her only from what she remembers of him in the past when he was alive. As she calls him into the present world, it is a world he no longer inhabits or knows about.)*

DAD. And I do love you, Evangeline…always…no matter what happens…remember that…

ANGIE. Daddy?

DAD. Evangeline?

ANGIE. Listen – I have no one else to tell this to –

DAD. Now while I'm gone to war – be a good girl, hear? Go to church. Pray to God – who's gonna help you through. And listen to your Grandma. She's gonna take care of you fine –

ANGIE. She hasn't felt right for a long time to tell the truth. And I can't let Clarice know one thing. You know how you hated her and she was so selfish and you never trusted her? Well, nothing's changed! And I can't let Grandma know anything either on account of she can't take it anymore Daddy.

DADDY. Now Grandma's not so young anymore, so mind her real good and help her out.

ANGIE. I just lied to her – and I hate to lie to her! But I – I don't want to break her heart. I'm afraid to hurt her – she's getting frail Daddy – it's scaring me and –

DAD. *(interrupting)* Grandma's gonna be strong for you, Evangeline 'til I get back from War. She'll be your rock. But don't lean too hard –

EVANGELINE. I shouldn't even be at that dumb "preppie" school except I got zoned in because she wouldn't sell our place when that throughway got a contract to –

DAD. *(interrupting)* Why – at that school – when you're a big girl? You're gonna be a runner like your Daddy – in the satin uniform they'll put you in – blue and gold! You're gonna "run like the wind."

ANGIE. Can you understand something? They don't give out satin uniforms anymore! YOU HAVE TO BUY THEM YOURSELF! I'm the poorest kid, Daddy. It's rich guy's school now. Everybody buys their own gear – but me. And I don't know –

(Phone rings.)

GRANDMA. *(V.O.)* Angie?

ANGIE. *(calling down:)* I'll get it, Grandma! Stay in bed!

*(She turns to **DADDY**.)*

ANGIE. I have to go…

(He is gone. She goes down ladder, phone rings.)

GRANDMA. *(V.O.)* Angie?

ANGIE. I'm getting it!

(She runs into trailer, returns to porch with phone, not wanting to be overheard.)

Yes – this is Angie – well – I – I wasn't feeling well – I – the – the school nurse wasn't around when I left. My Grandma? Well – she – she's at a church meeting tonight…Me? Tomorrow? Principal's office – 9 a.m. –

(She clicks off.)

ANGIE. *(cont.)* Oh-mi-God!

GRANDMA. *(V.O.)* Who was it, honey?

ANGIE. Wrong number. Go back to sleep –

(Blackout. Lights up school office. Next day. **THEO**'s *copying, pulling sheets from copier, stacking them in piles. He stacks elaborately, twisting and flipping pages. as he goes.* **ANGIE** *enters, watching.)*

THEO. Now "A"'s on top and "B"'s next down
And then there's "C" and you flip 'em all around.

(He flips pile on desk.)

Then "D" is fourth, and "E" is next
And that's one-eighth of the 9th grade class.
Now –

(Seeing **ANGIE**, *he turns to desk, embarrassed, busies himself.)*

ANGIE. I – I'm Angie Trublood?

*(***THEO*** doesn't turn around.)*

Principal just told me you were in charge here – volunteering time –

(Silence. Then:)

"Computer Whiz," he said.

*(***THEO*** keeps stacking papers.)*

I'm – I'm in here to work rest of the week…this last period…so – whatever you want me to do –

(He keeps stacking, restacking paper.)

(trying to ease the situation) I'm – on detention – skipping school…principal must've told you that…?

(He keeps shuffling papers.)

I – I can use a computer – but not too well. I could file though – only like not that way – I mean like flipping pages – rhyming – is that some trick to make it go fast?

THEO. *(not turning around)* Just a stupid way of amusing myself.

(an awkward silence)

ANGIE. *(seeing he can't cope with her in the office; handling the situation:)* You must be Teddy? That's what the principal said.

THEO. "Teddy Bear"?

*(**THEO** whirls around now.)*

That's what the man probably said, isn't that the case? That's usually the name that he employs.

ANGIE. Actually "Good Old Teddy Bear " is what he said.

THEO. A person could hate being called that!

(She looks at him, he at her.)

ANGIE. I'm sorry –

(beat)

THEO. Why? It's what *he* said. *They* said actually.

ANGIE. Who?

THEO. Jocks laid it on "Teddy Bear"! Gym class? Because I'm clumsy. Can't ordinate – slam dunk – anything! The coach let them name me that. "Hey! Here comes 'Teddy Bear' fumphun down the Court!" Coach laughed. Name stuck! A person could hate Jocks! Coaches!

(She laughs a little.)

ANGIE. They sure could…

(They connect again, looking at each other. He looks at her, thoughtfully, remembering something.)

THEO. You've negative experiences with athletics too… right?

(silence)

Here – you want a chuckle?

ANGIE. Tell me a joke you mean?

*(**THEO** pulls out package of candy. She takes one, he eats fistful.)*

I didn't know you meant candy…

THEO. Understandable. Because they give candy names on purpose that have *double entendres*.

ANGIE. Double what?

THEO. French. Means two meanings – one word. Advertizing gimmick. Promotes a product. They are Chuckles. You eat them, they'll make you happy and you'll "chuckle." And who doesn't want to be happy? Want another one? Try this flavor – the best. Makes you happy for sure.

(They both laugh, chew candy.)

Right?

(He pulls out another candy bag. they both take candy.)

THEO. Roll this around with your tongue. "Goo-ber." African for peanuts. Tastes – and feels like it sounds, doesn't it?

(He rolls candy in mouth:)

Cho-co-late and pea-nuts – "Goo-ber."

ANGIE. Sort of.

(She laughs a little. So does he.)

THEO. Onomatopoeia's the name for that. Know it?

ANGIE. Teacher talked about it - – I wasn't listening really –

THEO. "Skittles" is onomatopoeia too. Means bones – sounds like skeleton! "Skittles – Skeleton!"

(produces box of Skittles)

Looks like little bones

(He eats some.)

And "Gummy Bears"? Sounds mushy-chewy – like "gummmm"?

(He takes pack of gummies from pocket, eats one.)

ANGIE. You have so much candy!

THEO. They call me that: "The Gummy Geek."

(silence)

ANGIE. *(studying him, eyes linking:)* Anyone ever call you a name you like?

(beat)

Theodore?

THEO. Hate it. My father's name!

(Beat. She looks at him:)

ANGIE. What name then?

(silence)

THEO. *(looking down)* Theo. Never have been called it though…oh well – not true – not true. Brief encounter. Recently a guy from Iceland emailed me as: "Theo."

ANGIE. Theo. Its an unusual name.

(beat)

THEO. *(embarrassed)* Vincent Van Gogh's brother was Theo. Always liked him and his name

ANGIE. Vincent Van Gogh was a painter. I know that. But Theo Van Gogh?

THEO. He helped his brother, Vincent, get along…because – can you believe this – in his whole life Vincent Van Gogh sold only *one* painting! Theo got supported him, helped him through *everything!*

(Silence. She studies him, he looks up and they search each other's eyes again.)

Something wrong?

ANGIE. I don't like Angie either – sounds like a heart disease –

(They keep looking at each other. Connecting.)

THEO. *(Still looking at her, their eyes connecting. Then:)* Angela then?

ANGIE. Evangeline…my real name. My Daddy named me – found it in a book. But nobody calls me that except my Daddy does – did…

THEO. Did?

(beat)

ANGIE. He died…

(A silence. They are gazing at each other again. Something deeply connecting between them.)

THEO. Evangeline's a Greek name. Know what it means?

ANGIE. No.

THEO. "Little angel who brings good times and tidings to everyone."

ANGIE. *(affected, looking away)* Oh?

(looking back again)

What's Theo mean?

THEO. *(bursting into laugh)* Stupid meaning.

ANGIE. What?

THEO. *(cynically)* "A gift of God."

ANGIE. But that's a wonderful meaning!

THEO. To whom? In hot pursuit of that answer from day one!

(They search each others eyes.)

"Gift of God" to whom???

ANGIE. *(searching his eyes)* Your family?

(He starts stacking papers in elaborate manner.)

THEO. Let's file, let's file.

We'll make a pile!

And twirl the papers for awhile.

ANGIE. *(continuing to watch him)* You rhyme for different reasons, huh? Not just to amuse yourself and keep from getting bored. Right?

(He's silent, still turned away.)

I'm sorry – I didn't mean to pry. Not my business what you do or how – or even why you're here…

*(Silence as **ANGIE** picks up large pile of folders, puts them in drawers. Then trying to ease things for him and the awkward tension, and his embarrassment.)*

ANGIE. Well – in case you're wondering – I was supposed to try out for varsity – the 50 yard dash? Like I wanted to do it for my Grandma's sake. But I never even went to one practice…I don't look right…my gear – shoes – is what I mean. I just couldn't handle practice or the try-outs. I cut right out when it was my turn.

(She keeps filing.)

THEO. I saw you.

(She whirls around.)

ANGIE. ME?

THEO. School try-outs are open – everybody welcome on those bleachers. Theo goes. Lunch period? Nice day. Sun shining. Theo keeps informed –

ANGIE. *(embarrassed, turning away)* Oh-mi-God! You were there?

(beat)

THEO. *(quietly)* You looked all right…nice in fact – graceful – whatever you were wearing in the warm-up.

(She's turns away, embarrassed but pleased as he looks down, saying softly:)

If you went into training – practiced? I – I bet you could make varsity…and run like the wind –

(She looks at him startled.)

I say something wrong?

(Silence. Then:)

ANGIE. *(softly)* Someone else said that about me is all –

(beat)

THEO. Well, you could, I bet –

ANGIE. The girl's coach doesn't really want me in varsity anyhow. I'm like invisible in that gym.

THEO. INVISIBLE?

ANGIE. She sucks up to the rich girls. And seems like everybody's rich! It's like they're the ones make varsity. She coaches golf at Grassy Knoll Country Club – where all their folks belong.

THEO. Like my parents. They hang out there – after work – week-ends – golf – swimming – drinking –

(Bell rings.)

ANGIE. It went so fast. I'm sorry – I haven't helped you with anything –

THEO. *(looking at her)* Yes…you have…

(She starts out.)

ANGIE. *(looking back as they both smile a little:)* Well, peace out…Theo –

(He looks away.)

Something wrong?

(He looks at her, their eyes linking.)

THEO. Nothing –

(She exits. He is excited. He stuffs candy in his mouth, hurries from school area to his kitchen. Lights up. He tweeks birdcage.)

Now listen, Speckles? She is brave! Spunky! She came back to school on her own! For a detention she didn't even deserve!

(starts pacing, stuffs candy)

WHO WOULDN'T LEAVE THAT STADIUM UNDER THE CONDITIONS OF THINKING THEY DON'T LOOK RIGHT? WOULD BE MADE FUN OF?

(pacing faster)

And who says she doesn't look right? I noticed her! In warm-ups! Lots of girls running, jumping – but she's the only one with long hair flying. Long slender arms – legs – like she was almost flying, Speckles! Know what I mean? Huh? Huh? She's the one caught the eye

(stops looking at bird)

Know what else? It's like we know each other already – like we've talked personally about stuff before – gone through things together before when we haven't actually – we understand each other somehow, Speckles – in some deep, spiritual way…

(He feeds seed to Speckles, eats candy, paces:)

THEO. *(cont.)* It's a spiritual name actually – Evangeline. She liked –

(pause)

Hey, hey, hey! GOOGLE!

(He goes to laptop, flips it open, punching keys.)

"Evangeline"! Henry – Wordsworth – Longfellow" – it's a Prehistoric poem practically – a classic, Speckles, so it has to be here – public domain – free download – Yup! "EVANGELINE"! It's there! Now which font? Which font? Fancy! Fancy Olde English font! And away we go!

(looks over at Speckles)

Gonna make a nice cover with colored graphics for it too, Speckles! Use all this know-how Teddy Bear's stored up for something for a change!

(BLACKOUT. LIGHTS UP on trailer. ANGIE on roof in center of the circle of trophies, holding flag. Candles lit.)

ANGIE. *(singing in upbeat, happy way)*
Roses are red, my dear,
Violets are blue –

(Silence as she looks around.)

Daddy? Come! I have something special to tell! VERY SPECIAL! PLEASE COME HERE!

(silence)

Roses are red, my dear,
Violets are blue –

DAD. *(from far away)*
Angels in heaven
Know I love you!

*(**DAD** appears.)*

ANGIE. *(bursting with excitement)* Oh Daddy! Listen? There's a boy at school – a certain boy –

(beat)

DAD. Always remember, Evangeline – when my girl grows up, she'll meet a boy that's very fine

ANGIE. Now – you have to understand: he's way weird – like I mean not *weird* exactly. Strange – well, maybe not *strange* exactly – but not like other boys – he talks funny – not like "ha-ha" funny. Peculiar – well, not *peculiar* exactly – different –

DADDY. And he'll be a kind and gentle boy –

ANGIE. He knows so much! Like genius! Awesome actually. Computer, poems, art – definitions – everything there is to know about words actually.

DAD. He'll be a wonderful boy – the boy my girl will meet –

ANGIE. He doesn't know it, but – well, I have noticed him before. The bus? He won't sit down. Afraid he won't look right in the seat or the person next to him will say something rotten. I bet. He's way scared of lots of things, I think. But he's cool…

DAD. But most of all – he'll appreciate and accept and understand my girl! He'll see how beautiful she is…

(A silence. ANGIE gazes thoughtfully at him. Then:)

ANGIE. Daddy?

DAD. Evangeline?

ANGIE. Was my Mama beautiful to you? In her person? In her heart?

(pause)

DAD. Your Mama was the most beautiful girl I ever saw. In her person…in her heart. Had the voice of a nightingale too when she played her sweet guitar…

(silence)

ANGIE. *(looking thoughtfully at him a moment)* Maybe – maybe if I could find her now – if…

DAD. She turned on us and left, Evangeline. You were a baby. She ran out on you.

ANGIE. There's a TV show every day, Daddy – *The Finder?* They help people – sometimes they do a segment where they help teens find lost parents – if you write your story in and they pick you…I even got a form in the mail to write in –

DAD. She's gone forever!

(Silence. She looks hard at him.)

ANGIE. But if I got on that show they'd help me find her – I saw them find some boy's Dad once, and they got reunited. *Right on the show!*

DAD. She changed!

ANGIE. She might've changed back again by now –

DAD. She betrayed us, Evangeline!

ANGIE. Maybe she wouldn't betray me now I'm big. They have a missing person's center on the show, helping –

(She moves away, thinking.)

If they could find her now – I could tell her all about this boy! *She'd* help me figure out what to wear, I bet. And what to say…how to behave…

DAD. Forget her, Evangeline! She's never coming back! Remember that –

(Blackout. Lights up. CLARICE's bedroom. Knoxville. Phone rings. CLARICE hurries in. She's just come home and wears waitress uniform, carries pastry box which she quickly sets down. She punches the speakerphone on.)

CLARICE. The Brewster Trublood residence. Am I audio?

(Lights up, corner of an office. MISS DUVAL sits at desk on phone.)

MISS DUVAL. *(smiling:)* Mrs. Trublood, this is Miss Duval? Social Services? We met at the clinic conference regarding Angie's Grandma?

(Beat. CLARICE opens pastry box, takes bite of pastry.)

CLARICE. When I came all the way up there one hundred and fifteen miles each way middle of my professional business day, you mean?

MISS DUVAL. Yes.

CLARICE. Well, it is the end of my professional business day at the present time, Miss Duval.

(She takes off high-heels. She has swollen feet and they hurt. She slides into her fluffy mules, takes another bite of pastry.)

MISS DUVAL. And don't think I'm not sorry to trouble you again, Mrs. Trublood. But – well – Grandma has been found walking close to the throughway –

CLARICE. SHE GOT HIT?

*(**MISS DUVAL** stands, carrying phone receiver with her.)*

MISS DUVAL. No, a motorist picked her up and brought her to headquarters. They notified us. And I wanted to call you.

CLARICE. *(starts removing make-up with cold-cream)* Isn't there anybody *there* can drive a car to get her home?

MISS DUVAL. Oh, they've taken her home already.

*(**CLARICE** takes off uniform, massaging her aching back.)*

CLARICE. Then to exactly what is this after hours call pertaining?

*(**CLARICE** puts on "lounging robe" faux mirabeau trim, tying it one way, then another. It's slightly tight.)*

MISS DUVAL. Well – she seemed so shaken up – and – well – confused? At the police station? So, our supervisor – well, she's recommending "Assisted Living" – for this family unit – at this time –

*(Beat. **CLARICE**'s wrapping turban around her head.)*

CLARICE. What's that mean?

MISS DUVAL. That she and your niece come live with you.

*(Silence. **CLARICE** glaring at phone, consuming rest of pastry in one gulp.)*

CLARICE. I'm up there first of every month on the nose with $25 cash! And 2 restaurant dinners – with *two* desserts *apiece*! To say nothing of a six pack of Mountain Dew! Which is *all* I can possibly do with the predicament festering up there!

(Beat. **MISS DUVAL** *starts pacing.)*

MISS DUVAL. Of course – Grandma'd have her Social Security – and your niece her vets' benefits.

CLARICE. That's tiddly of what'd it cost!

MISS DUVAL. You'd be entitled to an aide for Grandma. Four hours a day.

(Silence. **CLARICE** *is eating pastry but giving this her full attention.)*

CLARICE. Aide? But they are widely known, Miss Duval, to eat up every delicious morsel in your Fridgedaire!

*(***CLARICE*** *takes another pastry.)*

On top of which most of 'em have criminal records and come right in your house, stealin Dresden plates and bottles of Sarah Jessica Parker's perfume, "Lovely"!

(She squirts some on.)

And then? They run your phone bill up to the moon callin over at Tokyo or Omaha!

MISS DUVAL. Point of fact – I was on a Committee two years investigating that very thing.

*(***MISS DUVAL*** *looks around, making sure nobody's around. She grows softer, confidential:)*

Never finished it though – we've had to let lots of things just slide through the cracks – point of fact –

(She looks around more. Silence. **CLARICE** *puts down perfume. Moves closer to phone to hear this. It's interesting her.)*

CLARICE. Really?

*(***DUVAL*** *speaks close to phone, whispering, shielding her mouth as she speaks:)*

MISS DUVAL. Mrs. Brewster – if I can confide in you? You seem so sweet.

CLARICE. Exactly what I'm know for, Miss Duval.

MISS DUVAL. Well then – you see – field reports, hospital records, medical reports – many, many of those – well, they get lost – tied up in so much red tape we just can't get it to unwind to find them…

(She keeps looking around to make sure no one's listening.)

And I'm the one responsible for so many of the cases. Breaking my heart in two – like at your conference I mean – I felt so protective of you and yours.

(She rises, moves to corner of desk, sequestering herself.)

And well – there is simply not one living soul here I dare confide my feelings to – "not a professional attitude to have" they say – and I have so many feelings about what's going on here –

(She's choking up. Silence. CLARICE looking at speaker phone, thinking. An idea forming:)

CLARICE. Well – as you said, I am genuinely a sweet person. Actually widely known in Knoxville for my sympathy to every living soul and situation that comes my way.

(Silence. Then:)

MISS DUVAL. Oh, bless your heart! Well then – I ask for your sympathy about this – you read about that poor baby found in a trash bag last summer? Over at Runyon?

CLARICE. Mmm –

MISS DUVAL. *My* fault! I had no one to assign to "follow ups" over there. On the family I mean. They were under surveillance.

CLARICE. Terrible for you, Miss Duval –

MISS DUVAL. Breaking my heart!

(MISS DUVAL sits, about to break down. She wipes glass frames, blows nose. CLARICE thinking. Then:)

CLARICE. Can you hold on? Got a tea kettle on the boil –

(CLARICE gets up, starts pacing, thinking. MISS DUVAL composes self, looks around, opens file on top of many

others on desk, scanning it. Then **CLARICE** *speaks again. She's formed her idea:)*

CLARICE. Miss Duval – at the clinic last time – The conference you just mentioned – when we met.

MISS DUVAL. Yes?

CLARICE. After Dr. Franklin arrived – and you *left?*

MISS DUVAL. I had to drive way up at Valley Junction, on a field visit. No one else available.

(beat)

CLARICE. Well – Dr. Franklin confided to me then, in private, that they took tests on Grandma. You've seen those of course – ?

MISS DUVAL. Nothing ever came to this office at all! Oh Lord, Mrs. Trublood –

(She rifles through files on desk.)

There must be fifty other cases like that too! Incompletes! Medicals lost – case histories – misplaced – It's all just breaking my heart – like I said – tearing me in two!

(She's starting to cry again. Beat.)

CLARICE. *(conspiratorial, almost a whisper)* Well, don't have to break your heart over *this*, Miss Duval. As I will tell you exactly how those tests resulted: Grandma is an osteoporosis – and a confirmed Alzheimer!

MISS DUVAL. What?

CLARICE. Doctor asked for long term facility care immediately. Not "assisted living" with me! And *now?* She's almost got run over by who knows comes roaring down that throughway with motorcycles and tattooed arms? It's an emergency she get into long term!

MISS DUVAL. Oh dear! And I didn't even know!

CLARICE. And not just the doctor – now we know, it's what me and Brewster want too! We have Power of Attorney and Legal Guardianship in the situation, of course… you must be aware of *that* – ?

MISS DUVAL. Uh– well I didn't look up the case history – I –

(She now starts searching the stack of files, then opens desk drawers, looking.)

CLARICE. *(interrupting)* I'm sure you'd've been part of the discussion, if you were there – and known everything, just like I told Angie. But now? With Grandma's file lost – and your supervisor's apparent declaration of designation that Grandma live here without doctor's orders –

(Beat. **MISS DUVAL** *now clicks her laptop.)*

MISS DUVAL. Look, I'm phoning up Dr.Franklin's office number right now. We have to straighten this out. I can't let this slide by too! Hang on?

(She clicks on phone, dials number.)

CLARICE. SHOOT!

*(***CLARICE** *begins pacing.* **MISS DUVAL** *on phone to Doctor's Secretary.)*

MISS DUVAL. Social Services here. Miss Duval. Could you send over a duplicate of the medicals on Hannah Trublood. From a conference? Yes. Then. We've somehow misplaced them. Of course.

(a beat)

Really?

(She writes something.)

Yes. Monday? Thank you.

(She clicks back to **CLARICE.***)*

(Speaker phone)

Mrs. Trublood?

CLARICE. Yes?

MISS DUVAL. Doctor's secretary can't find any report either. Only a one sentence comment from Doctor about Grandma's iron deficiency.

CLARICE. Maybe *she* lost it.

MISS DUVAL. Doctor's gone to a conference but will call in Monday. I'll just wait 'til then on what he said.

(long silence)

CLARICE. I just told you what he said! And what an unnecessary shame if it came out in discussion with Doctor and me – since I would of course need to talk to him too – that it was *your* office lost all reports and, without any orders from *him, your supervisor* sent Grandma down here? Seems like heads might just roll around up there –

(silence)

MISS DUVAL. *(Frightened. Gets up, moving around, thinking fast. whispering:)* Look, I'll tell Supervisor what you told me about the diagnosis – and that *Doctor's secretary's* the one must've lost the reports – which may well have happened. Doctor's gone, so I'll suggest we get *special priority status* for Grandma for immediate long term. We'll line up a teen home for Angie too.

(beat)

CLARICE. Oh dear, someone's at the door. Excuse me again?

*(**MISS DUVAL** looks around. Sits, fixing her hair, straightening collar. **CLARICE** pacing, thinking. Comes back:)*

You know? I have to draw a line about Angie! A Veteran hero's orphan with delinquent drinkers and dopers? Why they carry who knows what sexual diseases right into the dining room where God knows how clean the silverware is with the cheap detergents *I* am knowledgeable they use!

(A very long pause. Then:)

We are close and loving kin – and Guardians of Angie! Her home will be with us! And if there's any problem with that, we would have to discuss the terrible mix-up on this entire case with all the folks up there...

(Silence. **MISS DUVAL** *makes a very tidy pile of her files. Then:)*

MISS DUVAL. I will persuade my supervisor that for the well being of our department and for extreme and extenuating circumstances on the case, we must skip *any* official department meetings on *any* of this and just sign off! Case closed! She listens to me, and I think she'll go along.

CLARICE. The future of destiny in your hands!

(Blackout. Lights up on trailer. **ANGIE** *running with letter.)*

ANGIE. *(excited)* Daddy! Come Daddy! Come! I want you again! Please come!

You'll never guess – never in a million years!

(sings)

Down in the valley –

The valley so low –

*(***DAD*** *appears.)*

Oh Daddy! They answered me! That TV Show I told you about? *The Finder.*

(reading:)

"Dear Miss Trublood: Your letter and questionnaire received. We are interested in your story. Send description of mother and picture if possible, together with any information on last known whereabouts. *The Finder.*

DAD. Remember this – your Mama left us forever.

ANGIE. But I have her snapshot in my locket –

(She touches locket she wears.)

ANGIE. *(cont.)* And that claim check from New York with her name tag. Her guitar they sent back.

(reading tags dangling from guitar case)

"Claim 6598. Port Authority Claims Dept., June, 1995" such a long time ago – "Sheryl Lynn Trublood. YWCA, 53rd & Lexington. New York." But maybe they keep files or something!

DAD. She left a note: "Take care a the baby. Sorry it never worked out – "

ANGIE. I DON'T WANT TO HEAR THAT NOW! DON'T!

*(She claps hands over ears. **DAD** leaves. She shinnies down ladder, into trailer, slams door.)*

(blackout)

*(Lights up. School office. **THEO** enters, takes something in gift paper from backpack. Hesitates. Puts it in desk drawer. **ANGIE** enters, he grabs files on desk.)*

ANGIE. You want me to help file again?

THEO. *(twirling files:)*

Now "F" is next

And "G"'s behind

And after that

"H" falls in line!

ANGIE. Those files I put in the drawer, Theo…?

(She opens drawer, pulls out gift.)

My name?

(reading:)

"Evangeline" – by Henry Wordsworth Longfellow – the title? And: "From Theo."

THEO. Famous poet: Longfellow. But 200 years old. So I guess he is "forget about it." Only American poet to have his statue in England though…Poets Corner… Westminster Abbey. He –

ANGIE. *(interrupting:)* "Evangeline's the name of a poem? My Daddy must've found this poem in a book somewhere –

(a beat)

THEO. Poem's too long. Not hot, or hip, or hop!

ANGIE. *(fingering pages, leafing through poem)* And you did it in this fancy print? And made this pretty cover? Thank you, Theo. What's it about?

(beat)

THEO. Just some plain people…people…Cajun farmers living in a place once – Arcadians in Louisiana. Had farms – land – villages – Gone now. Only memories of them left – good, strong American people – like the old timers here.

ANGIE. *(near tears)* I – I never owned a poem in my life, Theo…let alone with my name across the top as title –

(He shrugs. ANGIE, reading:)

This says it's "A tale of love – a woman's beauty and strength and courage – "

(She looks quickly at him then turns page.)

"This is the forest primeval –
The murmuring pines and
The hemlocks" –

(looks at him)

Not my birthday. Christmas. Anything! I don't even hardly know you – not really –

(They are looking at each other, connecting in some deep way.)

I'll put it away so nothing happens to it. Thanks again.

(Silence. He starts pacing:)

THEO. Well – a person deserves something. Hurt to pieces! Slipping away to nurse the wound of humiliation and failure! Prejudice for being different! And she gets punished for *that*? It's like a bird – pushed from its nest by the other birds because it looks DIFFERENT! Breaks its wing? Drags someplace to nurse itself. But is found –

(He turns away, trying to regain composure but he can't.)

THEO. And gets bitten, ripped, torn – because it's DIFFER-ENT!

(From his pocket he takes fistful of candy, shoves in his mouth.)

ANGIE. You have some bird or something – that got hurt…?

(beat)

THEO. *(nodding)* Speckles I call her – because she's speckled. Her parents and brothers and sisters pushed her from the nest because she was speckled – and they were gray.

ANGIE. And you love her very much?

THEO. Named her for a Bible quote – Jeremiah – 12 – 7 – 9: "Speckled bird – the – other birds are round about against her." Know it? There's even a song about her – "Great Speckled Bird."

(She is studying him. He meets her gaze as again they connect, searching each other's eyes.)

ANGIE. Speckles and you are in a house on the hill – those fancy "Grassy Knoll Estates," like the other kids from school, huh? Must be real nice to live in a mansion up there…

THEO. Live? Well, "live" is defined as 1): "to flourish in human life." And/or 2): "to occupy not a house but a home." And/or 3): "to outlast danger."

ANGIE. Oh?

THEO. So, in answer to your question, Theo'd say "no" to the first two. But as to 3? Yes! Theo is making the ultimate attempt to "outlast danger"! In his empty mansion on the hill…Theo is trying – to live!

(She looks at him. He at her, again searching each others eyes. Impulsively she takes his hand, holding it in both her own.)

(blackout)

(Lights up. Another day. Clarice's bedroom. She's getting dressed to go somewhere, talking to Brewster, in next room offstage, from which we hear TV.)

CLARICE. …So then Brewster – just 25 minutes ago – Miss Dimwit Duval calls *again* – And Brewster? She is so afraid I am gonna spill her beans about that messed up office of hers and that her and her Supervisor might get canned? She has already found a Facility for your Ma and is clearing the path to have Angie here –

(She looks towards next room.)

CLARICE. *(cont.)* You aren't drinkin beer *again* in there almost at the crack of dawn, are you Brewster? You are hearing this? Because this is reality news!

(The TV goes up a notch as she makes up.)

So. Then she starts talkin about how the school thinks the girl'd be better off with us too. And I go: *"School"*? And then she hits us a homer, Brewster! Because the school has told her Angie has skipped classes, never made *any* sports team at all, let alone varsity! And is on detention besides!

(She moves toward other room.)

Brewster, why don't you stop listening to those "Wheel of Fortune" reruns when I am revealing to you how living Fortune is spinning right out of the TV and onto our livingroom floor!

(TV goes up another notch. She goes back to getting ready, putting on a hat.)

"Well," Miss Dimwit goes on, "I spoke to my supervisor about *everything* – and the good news is we're recommending that you become Angie's *Legal Foster Parents*. See she doesn't know we're not even Guardians, Brewster. "Then," she says, "Besides her VA pension – there's a $300 allowance. Every single month!" Brewster, you listenin up? 'cause I have not even begun with our Fortunate Turning of the Wheel! "In addition," she goes on, "there's an allowance for NEW FURNITURE for her room!"

(She looks in the mirror, thinking a moment.)

And you know how I have always wanted a little girl of my own. And would get her a four-poster with a pink satin cover and pillows to match.

(pause)

Someone to care about me – tell me I'm pretty

sometimes – buy me a birthday card – give me a kiss – have a hot tub waiting for me when I get home – to soak my sorry feet...

(pause)

I just thought of something, Brewster. Instead of her stupid name out of some bygone book? I am gonna call her – "Little Clarice"! That's what I am gonna call that little girl!

(dons coat, moves toward other room)

So, come on! All we got to do is go up there, and walk the walk and talk the talk! We'll get that girl right off the roof, into the truck, and bring her *home*! Just scoot on up and –

(She looks into other room.)

SLIPPED OUT ON ME? I am talkin to nobody? And have to take the bus all by myself? Whole damn family is WACK-A-DOO!

(She starts off.)

Well! Hell or high water, I am gonna make an exemption of Little Clarice!"

(blackout)

End of Act One

ACT TWO

(Later. Lights on **ANGIE** *on roof, reading:)*

ANGIE. "Fair was she to behold
   This maid of 17 summers
   And black were her eyes…and her hair.
   And fair was this maiden to see –"

*(***CLARICE*** enters.)*

CLARICE. Angie?

ANGIE. Aunt Clarice!

CLARICE. Found her wanderin the throughway, huh?

ANGIE. She was on the shoulder of the side road. She went to the mail box and it was a nice day, and she wanted to take a little walk.

CLARICE. Tell it to the Marines! Gonna get you a job writin "Spin City 2" for CBS is what I'm gonna do!

ANGIE. Someone drove by and didn't know who she was or what she was doing. So they stopped. That's all it was!

CLARICE. That "someone" found her wanderin the throughway! And 9ll was called again! And Miss Dim Wit called *me* again! And I am here to tell you I am too burdened with my own hindrances to keep coming up here over and again on account of your Grandma's Brain State!

*(***ANGIE*** climbs down from roof.)*

ANGIE. She's doesn't have a "brain state" for God's sake!

CLARICE. Don't contradict me. I told you she did before. And she does now! And don't use the Lord's name in vain and be impolite to every religion at large! Your Grandma needs proper attention now in long term care.

ANGIE. What're you talking about?

CLARICE. Of which I have come to inform her. And for which she is eligible and they have a place all lined up. And I will sign her in.

ANGIE. You joking me?

CLARICE. Brewster's next of kin and both of us are legal guardians for you and her. In addition that Miss Dimwit has demanded, on Dr. Franklin's advice and consent, your Grandma get immediately into that long term. And you come live with us and be *our* little girl. I am gonna be your mama now!

ANGIE. WHAT?

CLARICE. And I am hopin you'll love your new Knoxvolle school so much, you won't *ever* think of cutting – which they told Miss Dimwit you have done when she called your school.

ANGIE. She called my school?

CLARICE. Doesn't matter because you won't be there anymore. Or sittin here on a tin roof singin like a Looney Tune! You'll be in Knoxville in the healthy climate of our home.

(*Long silence. Then:*)

ANGIE. You really mean this?

CLARICE. Where you'll be regular. Do homework. Wear pretty dresses and help me out with laundry and ironin.

ANGIE. WHAT?

CLARICE. Then Saturdays? I am gonna get you a wonderful opportunity: "Part Time Kitchen Assistant!" Where you'll have your *own money* – CDs, a cell, movies, make-up!

ANGIE. You want me to work in your restaurant?

CLARICE. Well, I'm hopin I can persuade them. Then – when you graduate? Maybe we can wrangle you a "full hostess shift!"

ANGIE. I want to go to college!

(**CLARICE** *doesn't hear; lost in her fantasy.*)

CLARICE. Big-time salary for you then – clothes – perfume – good looking shoes – and I won't charge you one cent of rent – so you'll have more to spend! You'll be with me always at that wonderful Crystal Cafe.

ANGIE. I can't believe you're actually saying these things!

CLARICE. And we are gonna get rid of that Dinosaur name you got stuck with too: Evangeline! We are gonna start callin you "Little Clarice!" Now how's that?

ANGIE. You must be crazy! That's not my name! You're not my mother! And I'm not going to Knoxville! My home is with my Grandma! Here!

CLARICE. Your Grandma's on borrowed time, Miss.

ANGIE. The doctor would've said! He knows I'm alone here with her.

CLARICE. I think he must've wanted to break it to you easy. But she is an authentic Alzheimer. He confided that to me at the Conference. Didn't I tell you that then?

ANGIE. STOP THIS! I WON'T –

(GRANDMA comes out.)

GRANDMA. Clarice.

CLARICE. *(sweet voice)* Well. How you doin, Ma?

GRANDMA. You were just here. Why'd you come?

CLARICE. That Miss Dimwit Social Worker? Called twice! I talked to Doctor Franklin too. On account of you roamin around on the throughway! They both asked me to get on up here and talk to you. "Extenuating and Extreme Emergency Situation" was their very phrase.

GRANDMA. I went for a walk.

CLARICE. *(holding up bag)* Mmm. Well – I brought you all fried chicken, Ma…and coconut pie! And your favorite: Mountain Dew! That oughta make you feel better – calm you down –

ANGIE. We have food.

CLARICE. This *here's* restaurant food! Nutritious! Skinny as you are!

(*looks at her*)

CLARICE. (*cont.*) Bet you're the one cookin – or – openin the cans of beans! Not Grandma!

(ANGIE *and* GRANDMA *exchange quick looks.*)

ANGIE. That's not true!

CLARICE. Well I know she's not providing supervision anywhere else – as concerns your school for example –

(ANGIE *looks quickly at* CLARICE, *then* GRANDMA)

GRANDMA. She's doing fine at school.

(*Beat.* CLARICE *looks at* ANGIE.)

CLARICE. Well – sad as it is – I guess you better just know the truth, Ma.

ANGIE. STOP!

(GRANDMA *looks at* ANGIE.)

GRANDMA. What're you talkin about Clarice?

CLARICE. Angie's commenced cutting school.

GRANDMA. What?

ANGIE. STOP I SAID!

CLARICE. Day of those try-outs a while back? When you fell and I came up here – when she came home early?

GRANDMA. Teacher Conference Day?

CLARICE. It was a school day. And she *cut* – and is serving a detention sentence to this *very minute* on account of her truancy!

(*beat*)

GRANDMA. That true?

(ANGIE *turns away.*)

Angie?

CLARICE. And she never made varsity, either – painful as I know that is for you to tolerate, Ma. She lied to you. And she –

ANGIE. (*cutting in*) WILL YOU STOP?

CLARICE. She didn't even try-out because she never even went to practice, not even –

ANGIE. STOP IT! STOP IT! STOP IT!

(ANGIE grabs CLARICE, shaking her.)

GRANDMA. ANGIE! *You* stop it and apologize!

(ANGIE lets go.)

Apologize!

ANGIE. I'm sorry.

GRANDMA. That true Angie? What Clarice says?

(Silence. ANGIE turns away. GRANDMA sits heavily in rocker.)

GRANDMA. Where'd you get this from Clarice?

CLARICE. Social Worker called the school.

GRANDMA. How come?

CLARICE. Look, Ma. All of us're just tryin their best to solve The Emergency Situation that has arrived here: Social Worker. And Brewster, and *me*!

(ANGIE glares at her. A beat.)

GRANDMA. What exactly is it everybody's got in mind as "The Emergency Situation," Clarice?

(pause)

CLARICE. Well – Dr. Franklin has imparted to Brewster and me – confidentially – that you are in need of a long term nursing Facility, Ma. You need professional surveillance – which is not possible here. Like in that Keota Terrace that has a vacancy they discovered. Such a beautiful place!

(GRANDMA looks at her.)

And then Social Services says Angie's to comes live with us.

ANGIE. Grandma, I don't want to. I –

CLARICE. *(cutting in)* Brewster's willin to more than try 'n take her Daddy's place. Drive her up to see you every chance he gets! 'n I'd get her such pretty flowery little dresses. Designer jeans. Send her to the best school in Knoxville! And decorate a room for her with a brand new *four poster bed and pink spread* – where she could bring her girlfriends and –

(ANGIE runs and puts her arms around GRANDMA.)

ANGIE. *(cutting in)* She's gonna call me "Little Clarice" and make me call her "Ma" and work in her rest –

CLARICE. *(cutting in)* I am tryin my leveled best for all concerned with the orders from the County and the writing I have found on these sorry walls!

(Silence. Another. GRANDMA looks from CLARICE to ANGIE.)

GRANDMA. Clarice – go along home – I need to think things through –

CLARICE. Nothing to think through. Like to see you all agree to what's happenin, rather than create a forced event! That's all I –

GRANDMA. *(interrupting:)* Took the bus, didn't you? Last local back to Knoxville stops here quarter past as I recall – almost that now –

(Beat. Another.)

CLARICE. Well – I will be waiting for your call, Ma – and I just know you're gonna say you're goin to Keota Terrace. And that you'll be more than happy to see us do right by that little girl!

(CLARICE exits as ANGIE starts to roof.)

GRANDMA. Angie, stop!

(ANGIE stops.)

What's happened at school?

ANGIE. I don't know

GRANDMA. Don't know?

ANGIE. I didn't want to upset you.

GRANDMA. So you lied?

(*silence*)

Answer me!

(*Silence. Then:*)

ANGIE. (*blurting out:*) All right! You want the truth? I don't have the right clothes! Or shoes!

GRANDMA. I got you stuff to wear.

ANGIE. For varsity? That "Rummage Rag" stuff?

GRANDMA. What?

ANGIE. That's what the girls call me in what you got. You know that? The locker room! The Track! EVERY-WHERE! "Hey 'Rummage Rag'!"

GRANDMA. You're lettin' what you wear get you down? Make you start lyin' to me? Cuttin' school? Where's your spunk?

ANGIE. Beat-up second hand canvas sneakers! Big boxer shorts from God knows where! Down to my knees! Boy's aren't they? They've got a fly! From the bottom of the heap of some church tag sale where you're always pickin through junk?

(*beat*)

GRANDMA. I am stretchin our money far as I can for you!

ANGIE. Other kids have six, eight pair of Nikes, Pumas, Adidas! Just to wear to class! They've got iPods, cells – designer jeans – credit cards for God's sake! They make fun of everything about *me*! You know that? My BUCK TEETH? And like I told you about a thousand times how I need braces and have to keep my upper lip over these crooked things so they won't show! Like this?

(*She pulls upper lip over teeth.*)

GRANDMA. STOP THAT! We've got what we got and –

ANGIE. *(cutting in)* But they show anyhow! So – "Squirrelly Girl" is what they call me too! And "Trailer Trash" – when they see me get off the bus for this shacky rattletrap!! Why don't *you* get me a house and designer jeans and a cell?

GRANDMA. *(cutting in)* I told you Angie I am –

ANGIE. *(clapping her hands over her ears)* SHUT UP! YOU JUST SHUT UP ON HOW YOU'RE *TRYING AND TRYING AND TRYING!!* I AM SICK OF HEARING IT!! I DON'T WANT TO HEAR IT ONE MORE TIME! GODDAMN IT TO HELL! I –

*(**GRANDMA** slaps her face.)*

GRANDMA. Get in the house!

ANGIE. *Trailer* you mean?

GRANDMA. Get in your bed!

ANGIE. *(starts climbing to roof)* NO! NO! NO!

GRANDMA. Now!

ANGIE. I WON'T! I WON'T! I WON'T!

*(Up the ladder **ANGIE** goes, **GRANDMA** coming after her, but **GRANDMA** stumbles, falls, clutches ladder, pulling herself up. Limping, she moves to rocker, **ANGIE** scrambles down.)*

ANGIE. I'm sorry! Oh–mi–God! You break your ankle? Oh-mi-God!

(a beat)

GRANDMA. Twisted a little bit's all – doesn't really hurt –

*(**ANGIE** kisses her. Silence. **GRANDMA** holds her at arms length now, studying her.)*

But –

(more silence)

ANGIE. What – ?

(longer silence)

GRANDMA. *(her eyes never off **ANGIE**)* There's years ahead –

(silence)

ANGIE. What are you talking about?

(Silence. **GRANDMA** *looks out past their yard.)*

GRANDMA. *(more to herself:)* Be one thing – then another – then another –

ANGIE. Huh??

GRANDMA. *(still more to herself:)* First time this kinda thing happened with you – school – me – won't be the last –

ANGIE. Nothing'll ever happen again! Anywhere! Anytime!

GRANDMA. Grandma loves you deep, sweetheart – you're her whole family – her whole life now –

ANGIE. I love you too, Grandma. Your my whole family too. And I'll be good. Swear to God!

(She hugs and kisses her.)

GRANDMA. And teen years is tough – someone tough's got to see you through 'em...so you make somethin of your life. That's what I want for you. And I'm not tough enough to count on gettin you through...not anymore –

ANGIE. YOU ARE! YOU ARE!

GRANDMA. *(looking at her now)* Aw, darlin – can't you see? We *can't* count on me – we don't know what the next day's gonna bring for the old lady, sweetheart – do we?

(Silence. Then **GRANDMA** *rises, starts to trailer.)*

I'm callin' Clarice, Angie. Tell her we agree on what she wants: I'll go on into a home – and you'll go live with them right away. No force. No commotion. I sure don't want that!

ANGIE. OH-MI-GOD, NO!! I WON'T!!! GRANDMA NO!!!

GRANDMA. You will, Angie! Hard choice for both of us, but it'll be best for you. We both of us have to trust God it will, sweetheart – and then *you* have try real hard to make that choice be best. Hear?

(She is starting to cry. Not trusting herself to look back, she exits to trailer as **ANGIE** *climbs frantically to roof.)*

ANGIE. DADDY! Something terrible's happenin' – DADDY? DADDY!

(She pulls out guitar frantically singing:)

Down in the valley

The valley so low –

(DAD appears.)

ANGIE. *(cont.)* Oh thank God! Daddy, Grandma's letting Clarice put her in a facility and take me away! And I've never asked you to do anything for me – just to listen – to be with me. But you have to help me now! You have to DO THINGS! FIGHT THIS OFF!

DAD. I'll always be with my little girl. Always.

ANGIE. That's not enough. You've got to help me stop Grandma! And Clarice! NOW!

DAD. When I get back from War, Evangeline – we're gonna be together always – do things together always –

ANGIE. NOW! DO THINGS NOW! Quick! STOP CLARICE!

(silence)

ANGIE. DO IT! HELP ME NOW!

(silence)

WHY DON'T YOU ANSWER?

(beat)

DAD. You'll be by my side – me guidin' you – my *little girl.*

ANGIE. *(looking at him startled, with dawning awareness:)* But I'm not little ! I'm almost all grown up! You have to guide me *now!*

DAD. You want to sing our song?

(beat)

ANGIE. Don't you understand?

DAD. "Down in the valley

The valley so low –

Hang your head over – "

Don't you want to sing with Daddy, sweetheart?

(long silence)

ANGIE. *(looking at him a long time, then whispering)* You can't help me – can you? There's nothing you ever can do for me –

DAD. When I come back from war –

ANGIE. *(backing off, scrutinizing him)* But you – you never came back from war – you're *dead!*

(Beat. Several more. She turns away, grappling with what she realizes. Then resolved:)

ANGIE. Leave me! Never come again!

(He begins to retreat.)

I love you...I'll remember you forever – but you're only a memory –

(He's gone. She stands alone. Lights down on her, up on school. THEO at computer. Glances at watch, gets up, looks down hall, returns, eats candy. ANGIE enters.)

ANGIE. *(head down)* Sorry I'm late – I'm –

THEO. Thought maybe you got sick –

ANGIE. Should I finish alphabetizing?

THEO. *(looking at her)* Okay –

(She puts backpack on desk, takes papers, alphabetizing, not looking at him.)

Hey?

(silence)

What's up?

(silence)

Jock girls on your case?

(no response)

Principal?

(no response)

Just one too many days Solitary Confinement Punishment with The Gumdrop Gweep! Right?

(He stuffs fistful of candy in mouth.)

ANGIE. *(flashing him a look)* It's not you – so don't put your-self down. Okay?

THEO. That Stone Age poem then? Stupid *long*-hair, *Long* - Fellow!

ANGIE. I like that poem!

(She pulls poem from backpack.)

I carry it everywhere…

(THEO starts typing on computer.)

THEO. *(looking up at her)* Then what's wrong?

ANGIE. *(blurting out)* Cut me a break? You think it's easy for me? And that if something goes wrong for me, it must be you?

THEO. I – I didn't mean to say –

ANGIE. *(interrupting)* I am trying to "outlast danger" too, Theo. If you want to know. To "live" like what you told me the definition means. Evangeline's also making "the ultimate attempt" like you called it. But is failing – if you want to know! Has failed in fact!

THEO. What's that mean?

ANGIE. I only came in here to say goodbye.

THEO. What?

ANGIE. She moves very fast to get what she wants. My Aunt Clarice. She got them to take Grandma to a clinic this morning. For a day of tests. Then she's going right into a long term facility. And Grandma? She actually thinks it's for the best!

THEO. What kind of tests?

ANGIE. Alzheimer's…

THEO. But that takes a long time to diagnose –

ANGIE. I don't know – she's already been diagnosed, I think – What I know is Clarice is picking me up to go live with her in Knoxville! Today! Be "A Part Time Kitchen Girl" called "Little Clarice"!

(She moves away.)

It's the end of any dream.

THEO. Whose dream?

ANGIE. *(near tears)* Grandma's – mine – in our broken down trailer – with a dream that's gone…there was just us…I already told you my – my Daddy – died –

(silence)

ANGIE. *(cont.)* I'm trapped now –

(She turns away, hiding tears. Several beats. Then:)

THEO. *(almost to himself)* "Died – does – did–"

(Silence. **ANGIE** *turns around.)*

ANGIE. What?

THEO. When you told me your Daddy called you Evangeline –

ANGIE. What about it?

THEO. You said: "he *does* call me Evangeline " – like he was alive. Then you said: "He *did*" – and now? "He *died*."

(Beat. Then:)

ANGIE. So?

THEO. Well – it's like – he was dead *and* alive – at the same time – …

(A long silence. She looks at him. He locks eyes with her. Softly:)

You – you know I talk to my Speckles…right? And Samaritan my little cat – all my animals in fact – and they understand – you know that, don't you? I do weird – mystical things – with them – because I *know* they understand me – and I understand them –

(Silence. Then:)

ANGIE. *(whispering, head down)* I – I talked to my dead Daddy – because – he wasn't dead – to me – you're right – he understood – I could even see him –

(whispering more softly:)

He came to me…on my roof…

(looking at him from corner of her eye:)

You – you get what I'm telling you?

(a beat)

THEO. *(softly)* Yes –

ANGIE. I – I've never told another soul this on this earth – it's way, way weird –

(Silence. Then:)

THEO. What'd you talk to him about?

ANGIE. Everything.

THEO. Like Speckles and me – I tell her everything…

ANGIE. But it's so over. Daddy – Grandma – the trailer… Soo over! Soo yesterday!

(beat)

THEO. *(looking at her)* Why can't you just stay there with your Mom?

(beat)

ANGIE. There is no Mom. She ran out on me when I was a baby, Theo, to New York. Never gave me a chance. But I always figured she'd like to live with me if I was grown up. And now I am. You know? There's a TV Show that finds lost parents… *The Finder* – if I could only get to talk them – and get on the show and if they could –

(Suddenly she runs out.)

THEO. Evangeline? Hey? Where you going? Hey, Evangeline?

*(Lights out. Up on trailer as as **THEO** runs in. Almost evening. Stops at sight of trailer. Dingy, abandoned with "For Sale" sign on it. Knocks.)*

Evangeline?

(He looks around, sees broken trophy on ground, head of figure off. Picks up pieces, reads inscription. With statue starts to his own kitchen area, talking to self:)

Should've stopped her in the office! STOPPED HER! DUMB ASS! Stupid! STUPIDO! She was trying to tell me *something!*

*(Lights on **THEO**'s kitchen. He enters, goes to Speckles.)*

Oh God! OH GOD! Speckles? Where'd she go? She told me her Mom had left her to go to New York…"if only I could" she said – "if"…

*(Light out. Up on new area: corner of Bus Station. **ANGIE** sits with guitar case. As:)*

STATIONMASTER. *(V.O.)* Departing Gate # 1: Atlanta, Chatanooga, Knoxville, Gate #!. Atlanta, Chatanooga, Knoxville. Gate #1.

*(Announcement keeps droning on under **ANGIE** who pulls out letter reading to self:)*

ANGIE. "Dear Miss Trublood –

STATIONMASTER. *(V.O.)* Gate #1: Departing. Atlanta, Chatanooga, Knoxville. Boarding now open Gate #2: Tulsa, St., Louis, Chicago, Cleveland –

ANGIE. "…Producers of "The Finder" are pleased to tell you, you have been selected for a preliminary interview for our spring series of "The Finder." We would like to talk to you at our studios in New York. Please bring with you any information – documents, pictures, addresses concerning your Mother. We would –

STATIONMASTER. *(V.O.)* Change in Cleveland for Erie and Port Authority Terminal, New York City, New York.

(She looks up at word: "New York")

STATIONMASTER. *(V.O.)* Gate #2. Now boarding.

*(**ANGIE** stuffs letter in pocket, rises, slings guitar case over shoulder, looking around for Gate #2.)*

STATIONMASTER. *(V.O.)* Now arriving Gate #3. Greyhound from Detroit, Toledo, Columbus, Charleston, Beckly and Wyethville.

*(**THEO** enters bus station, stands at doorway looking around. Following together, overlapping:)*

Gate #4: Bus arriving from Oklahoma City, Norman, Dallas, Ft.Worth.

Abiline –

THEO. *(Calls softly, as "Abilene" is called, so he &* STATIONMAS-
TER *speak names in unison:)*

Evangeline – ?

STATIONMASTER. *(V.O.)*

ABILENE –

*(*ANGIE *looks up, as if: do I hear him?* THEO *moves around area calling:)*

Evangline?

*(*ANGIE *sees Gate #2, starts to bus, then stops suddenly, warily looking around for him. He spots her.)*

THEO. ANGIE! OH THANK GOD!

(hurries to where she is)

ANGIE. I thought I heard you!

THEO. DON'T GET ON THAT BUS!

ANGIE. Leave! I took Grandma's money from her purse and her drawer. Bus fare – a room somewhere. There's a program that'll find her and like I am out of here!

THEO. *(interrupting)* And like *if – if* the program could find your Mother – right? And like *if* she'd come be with you – it's like everything would be wonderful! Right? You wouldn't have to live in Knoxville – your mama would take care of you – you'd keep Grandma at home – and everybody'd live happily ever after!

ANGIE. GET OUT OF HERE!

THEO. That isn't going to happen! You're soo smart – and you can't see *that*? You'll never find your mother because she doesn't *want* to be found – or she'd've come back to you a long time ago! It's just your *wish*! And "if wishes were horses beggars would ride!" Webster's dictionary, quote: "a wish: something one wants, desires, longs for" – a kid's fantasy, Angie, is what a wish is. GET RID OF IT AND GET AWAY FROM HERE!

ANGIE. Peace out!

(She turns away to go to bus as he glares at her.)

THEO. Don't say that to me! And listen up? You and Grandma had a dream once, right?

(She shrugs, moving toward Gate #2.)

Be an athlete – like your Dad – "Run like the Wind" – get a scholarship – be somebody?

(She turns, looking at him.)

ANGIE. Forget about me – will you?

THEO. Not such a strange dream! Lots of families dream like that!

ANGIE. It's over!

THEO. "Dream" – second and preferred meaning – to Theo – "to scheme, plan to attain something." Third and also preferred meaning – to Theo: "to consider something as a *possibility*, to give *serious consideration* to"!

ANGIE. Doesn't matter what you say with all those words! Forget about it! I am out of here!

(She keeps moving as he follows her.)

THEO. Your dream's a "possibility," Angie! It only needs your "serious consideration" – you only have "to scheme and plan to attain" it! DON'T LEAVE! PLEASE?

(She looks hard at him now.)

You can make your dream happen – swear to God! Remember what the poem said about Evangeline? "The story of a woman's courage – "

(He gains courage himself:)

I–I want you to stay! I – I need you to, Angie! For *me?* Stay?

STATIONMASTER. *(V.O.)* FINAL CALL! GATE #2! Destination: Port Authority, New York City, New York! ALL 'BOARD!

*(**ANGIE** stops, turns and looks at **THEO** a long time.)*

ANGIE. *(whispering)* You mean it?

(He nods. She drops guitar, runs to him, embracing him. She is tearing, keeps head on his shoulder, holding tightly to him:)

ANGIE. *(cont.)* Then I'm going to try – like Evangeline in the poem, Theo! I'm going to try!

(They stay in embrace. He runs his hand through her hair, speaking softly to her:)

THEO. You'll need to talk to the doctor, Angie…and that Social Worker.

ANGIE. Yes…right…

THEO. Want me to call them for you?

(Silence. Then:)

ANGIE. I – I need to make the calls myself Theo – it's *my* Grandma – and *me* supposed to live in Knoxville – right?

(She pulls back, holding him at arm's length.)

It'd be so lame if *you* called for me. I have to do it for myself –

(Pause. Then he nods "yes.")

You have your cell?

(He pulls it from pocket, gives it to her.)

Got a pen – some kind of paper? Write the numbers down?

(He pulls these out of pocket. She calls.)

Information? Two numbers please? Dr. Robert Franklin…the office? Thank you.

*(She turns to **THEO** who writes.)*

848-192-4404

(back to cell)

And then – County Hospital–Department of Social Services?

*(turns to **THEO**)*

848-397-6000, extension 14.

(back to cell)

Thank you.

(Lights down on scene, up on trailer. **CLARICE** *sits on porch in* **GRANDMA**'s *chair, holding up compact mirror, arranging hair, one way then another.* **ANGIE** *runs in. Stops in her tracks at the sight)*

CLARICE. Well, Miss Queen, whose roof you on now? With me nearly out of my mind in concern while you have made the election to play hooky *again!* Just the minute I come to take you to Knoxville.

ANGIE. I'm not going to Knoxville.

CLARICE. Stop that foolishness now, Angie, and get your things? So we can close this gypsy caravan up for good and all and pull the curtain down!

ANGIE. This is my home, Clarice. And I'm staying in it. You have no power over me like you said and everyone thought. And you haven't got any <u>other</u> powers over me either! Grandma does!

CLARICE. You get those wack-a-doo notions sittin on some roof in the sun too long? Now I have to drive your Uncle's junkheap on that Throughway 115 miles! Through deep congestion! Get your things?

ANGIE. I got through finally – to talk to Dr. Franklin, Clarice. He was at the hospital – but he called me from there!

*(***CLARICE*** *rises.)*

CLARICE. Dr. Franklin?

ANGIE. He never signed any medical papers about Alzheimer's or a facility or anything else! Because he never gave that medial diagnosis. I got through to Miss Duval at Social Services, too.

CLARICE. Miss Dimwit?

ANGIE. She told me everything – about how things slide through cracks there – and she couldn't find anything so she just believed you – because you got her scared! She was sorry. She's talked it over with her supervisor and Dr. Franklin too! That's not dimwitted, Clarice – that's honest – and strong!

(CLARICE turns away.)

ANGIE. *(cont.)* YOU LIED! Tricked her – Grandma – me! To get what you wanted! – But know what? You're the dimwit, Clarice!

(Beat. CLARICE turns back.)

CLARICE. You are overcome with roof sun and don't know what's emanating from your mouth or you would never say such hurtful things. Let's go!

ANGIE. I'm staying here in my home, Clarice. Waiting for Grandma to come here today.

(ANGIE now goes past CLARICE to trailer, which she unlocks, opening door. CLARICE starts backing away.)

She'll be fine. An aide's coming to help now every day – if the government doesn't stop paying her! And Miss Duval's getting me extra money from aid to dependent children, too. If Grandma needs a facility? Miss Duval will help find me one.

CLARICE. And where will you be then, Miss? Because I will *never* give you the time of day – let alone a wonderful bedroom with a picture window, pink satin pillows and whole bottle of Jessica Parker's "Lovely" cologne!

(CLARICE turns, starts down the road. ANGIE calling after her:)

ANGIE. I'll be going to boarding school, Miss Duval says – if Grandma goes to a home – then college – I'll get scholarships – be an athlete runnin' like the wind!

(They now overlap:)

I won't ever be your "Little Clarice"! My name's Evangeline!

CLARICE. Well, of all the pure mitigated gall! Bayin the moon! Wack-a-doo like the rest of 'em – the whole she-bang!

(CLARICE exits. ANGIE pulls up "FOR SALE" sign, dumping it in trashcan by trailer. Sits on porch steps as THEO enters.)

THEO. Your Grandma here?

ANGIE. Any time. And Clarice left when I told her what I'd done.

THEO. Dreams *you're* starting to make happen, right?

(She looks at him, smiles, as does he. Then softly:)

ANGIE. You know a lot about peoples' wishes and dreams – huh?

(He turns away.)

(steadily looking at him) And you have one too – a big dream I bet – ?

(He nods, back to her.)

But you think it can't happen? Like I thought mine couldn't – ?

(He shrugs, not turning around.)

And Speckles can only listen – not really help at all –

(He nods, turns. They look at each other. She now whispers:)

I – I think I know your dream – I can hear it – feel it deep – now – this very minute – now!

(A beat. He looks away.)

You want to help me – like you help your strays…like that other Theo helped his brother. Hey – look at me?

THEO. *(Nodding. Whispering:)* I – I want you to "run like the wind," Evangeline – for you – your Daddy's memory – your Grandma – and –

(close to tears) I – I want it – need it for me – I – I told you that before – at the bus station –

(silence)

ANGIE. *(softly:)* But – it – it's still all *my* fight now, Theo. You already helped me – *I'm* the one has to practice now – learn to run – make that coach open the door to *me*. And I will…swear to God!

THEO. *(He can't help smiling:)* Some cool shoes, and running shorts and a top might help open that door a little – at rich guy's school –

ANGIE. We can't afford gear like that, Theo. Maybe next year –

(silence)

THEO. Look – it's important *now*. Gives you confidence. I was thinking about it –

ANGIE. You were?

THEO. One thing the Dentists Green do is give Candy Crud "Credit Cards"! To amuse himself with "objects" and never bother them!

ANGIE. Oh?

THEO. Shoes? Shorts? I'll charge them out – online. Open the door a little? Be part of something! Bring Speckles to the bleachers. Watch you practice in your cool gear. Totally awesome for me –

(Beat. Two. Then:)

ANGIE. *(Gently. Thoughtfully:)* Hey, Theo – ? Would that be opening the door – like really?

THEO. What?

ANGIE. I mean, it'd be their Credit Cards – like the *Dentists Green* would be opening the door for me, wouldn't they? Not you?

(He turns away, popping a gum drop in his mouth.)

You – you *could* open the door for me, though, Theo – you know – like when you gave me the poem? That opened the door a crack – because – I mean, like it came from *you* – to *me* –

(She pulls poem from her pocket looking at it. He jams fistful of candy from pocket in his mouth.)

Oh-mi-God! Don't eat any more candy? Like you're getting revenge on them – having the rottenest teeth in town? So they'll notice you – like: "Look at the holes in that son of mine's teeth!"

(He moves farther away.)

Listen to me, please? I – I know *you* deep inside – like you know me – I can read your thoughts. You have to get over your parents, Theo. They'll never change and pay attention to you. They are so over! A kid's "wish" – like you told me about my Mom. Like in reality? It's *your* teeth are rotting!

(He turns half around.)

And in the office at school? You're *volunteering*! You've just about computerized every area and category in the entire school. I mean, I've thought about it before – I mean, like the things you know how to do are totally awesome, Theo – like – like you are –

(He looks away.)

Only – you're like, "Hey make a joke of me, please?" You do that totally! Like letting the principal get off on you: "Hey, Teddy Bear"! When you are *helping him out! Monumentally*!!

(He moves slightly away.)

Other kids get paid doing office work!

(She comes close to him, touches his shoulder. Very softly:)

Make him pay *you*? Then *you* buy me that cool gear – that'd be *your* gift then – like the poem. And I – I'd think that was awesome – like it'd open the door – and I could like really "run like the wind" then –

(He turns to her and they look in each other's eyes, then **THEO** *takes* **ANGIE** *in his arms and they kiss very tenderly.)*

(Blackout. Lights up. School stadium. A later time.)

LOUDSPEAKER. *(V.O.)* And now – results for the statewide Varsity Competition, in the 50 yard dash, girl's division: #44, from Farragut High School: Linda Lee Lockworth, first; #14, from Fairoaks Consolidated Schools, Meredith Coons, second; #53, from West Central Consolidated, Evangeline Trublood, third –

(As **LOUDSPEAKER** *drones on,* **ANGIE** *in good uniform and shoes, comes on winded, sweaty, drinking bottled water. She holds a trophy. Sweat band around her head, #53 armband on arm. She leans against bleacher, panting, catching her breath.* **THEO** *enters from another way, carrying birdcage. They look at each other.)*

THEO. *(extremely happy)* Hey, hey, hey!

(He touches trophy, admiring it.)

That's the real thing!

ANGIE. It's only 3rd place!

THEO. *(laughing)* "Only"?

ANGIE. Don't laugh! I need first if I'm ever going to get a scholarship. Next time – wait and see.

THEO. By spring you'll practice outside – it's better –

ANGIE. It's better right now!

*(***ANGIE*** notices birdcage* **THEO** *carries. It's empty.)*

ANGIE. Hey – where's Speckles?

(beat)

THEO. She flew away.

ANGIE. YOU JOKING ME?

THEO. She was in her cage beside me on the bleacher –

ANGIE. But how –

THEO. *(interrupting:)* I don't know – all of a sudden I heard the cage door swing open – right after your meet – and I don't know how that happened because I always latch it. Speckles was still inside though. Her head cocked – looking right at me –

*(***THEO*** and* **ANGIE** *link eyes, smiling just slightly, with just a hint of some deep knowledge and a touch of conspiracy.)*

ANGIE. And then?

THEO. She just kept cocking her head at me – almost like "a wink."

ANGIE. "A wink"?

THEO. Then – and I didn't plan it – out of my mouth came: "go!" And she went! Out and over the stadium. Her wing totally fine!

(He looks up. **ANGIE** *too.)*

And then she disappeared.

(Their eyes link. They are both smiling.)

THEO. *(cont.)* The poet, Percy Byshee Shelley. 1821. The poem: "To A *Skylark*": "Hail to thee blithe spirit!" Definition of blithe': "showing a cheerful, contented disposition."

(They are both smiling at each other, then still smiling, they look up to the sky.)

ANGIE. Like in: "Happy" – maybe?

THEO. And like in, quote: "Lighthearted and filled with joy!"

(They keep looking up in the sky, arms entwined, almost as if they see and hear Speckles singing a clear and beautiful song.)

(blackout)

End of Play

COSTUMES

ANGIE wears make-shift athletic uniform comprised of large men's shorts and tee. To school she wears too big torn jeans and men's shirt, shirttail hanging out. Later she wears good athletic clothes.

THEO wears horn-rim glasses, drab cardigan and chinos and oxford shoes.

GRANDMA wears simple country clothes and sensible shoes. Print cotton dress with apron in some scenes. Simple robe.

DAD wears a camouflage War uniform and boots that could have been worn in any war.

CLARICE wears what she thinks are extremely attractive clothes. that show her off, although she's a little too plump, and they don't. As Hostess of the Crystal Café, she wears black short dress, frilly apron, very high heels. In home scene wears fluffy scuffs and polyester satin lounging robe with Mirabeau collar. At Angie's she wears wrap coat with faux leopard collar and faux leopard beret.

MISS DUVAL wears dark suit, light colored blouse beneath and glasses.

SET, SOUND, LIGHTS, PROPS

Play is not realistic. Sense of fluidity throughout.

An other-worldly quality to piece that should sift through the play beneath its surface. Piece has a strong fantasy element to it.

Unit set: simple. Platforms, steps, scaffolding as solution to denoting various locations – outside trailer; the attached porch; the roof; and corners of THEO'S kitchen, high school office, bus station, Miss Duval's office, and Clarice's home. Trailer can be stylized set piece.

Sound: important and integral to play. All VOICE OVERS are simply that. No characters onstage:

1. LOUDSPEAKER (VO) from athletic field

2. TV SOUND

Important there is SOUND and that it get progressively louder. Same as use of (VO) in scene above. CLARICE'S reaction to the ever louder sound, helps show her internal loneliness.

3. STATIONMASTER (VO) in bus station.

Rural country folk-songs suggested for pre-show and Intermission music. Maybe several. "Great Speckled Bird"; "Down in the Valley" should be used in play.

Lights: used to maximize (sometimes with cross-fades) effect of shifting scenes, locales.

Props: (minimal): guitar, sheet of paper (poem), birdcage, laptop, folders with papers, letter from TV program, suitcase, guitar case.

Great Speckled Bird

Public Domain

What a beau - ti - ful thought I am thin-king,__ Con - cer - ning the Great Speck-led

Bird. Re - mem-ber her name is re - cor-ded__ In the pa-ges of God's Ho-ly Word.

Jeremiah 12-9

Lyrics:

What a Beautiful thought I am thinking, concerning the Great Speckled Bird
Remember her name is recorded in the pages of God's Holy Word.
All the other birds beat hard against her,
Until she was thrown from her nest.
But that Great Speckled bird from the Bible
She's the one that The Lord He loves best.
And the others, so set dead against her,
How they envy that she has been blessed
To carry our spirits far upward
As skyward she lies from the rest.
She is spreading her wings for her journey,
She's going to leave by and by.
She will rise with her song and our spirits
And be gone in that glorious sky.

Down in the Valley

Public Domain

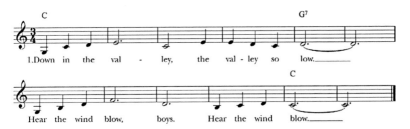

1.Down in the val - ley, the val - ley so low.

Hear the wind blow, boys. Hear the wind blow.

Roses love sunshine, violets love dew
Angels in heaven know I love you
Know I love you, dear, know I love you
Angels in heaven, know I love you.

ABOUT THE AUTHOR

SHIRLEY LAURO's latest play, *The Radiant*, about Marie Curie, and commissioned by Sloan Science Foundation, received its first workshop at The Actors Studio, June, 2009, starring Angelica Torn. Another recent play, *All Through the Night*, enjoyed its New York premiere at Off-Broadway's Marjorie Deane Little Theater, October, 2009. In Chicago's World Premiere the play received a Joseph Jefferson Nomination as "Best New Chicago Play of the Year" and subsequently was presented by Ashby Stages, Berkley, CA., and Traveling Jewish Theater of San Francisco. It is a Samuel French 2010 publication.

Clarence Darrow's Last Trial, recipient of an NEA "Access to Excellence" grant, a Carbonell nomination as "Best New Play in Florida, and The New American History Play Prize(finalist), is a Samuel French, 2010 publication as well – while her multi-generational play, *Speckled Birds*, will complete the trio of Ms. Lauro's 2010 Samuel French publications. *Audition* was produced at The Cherry Lane Theater, in the Festival: Turning Points, November, 2009.

Edited by Ms. Lauro with Alexis Greene, the anthology, *"FRONT LINES: Political Plays by American Women"*, enjoyed publication by New Press, June, 2009 and was chosen as an "Honoree of The Coalition of Professional NY Women in Arts and Media".

A Piece of My Heart, whose New York Premiere was at Manhattan Theatre Club, has enjoyed over 1,800 productions around the world, Recipient of the Barbara Deming Prize, The Kittredge Prize, The Susan Blackburn Prize(finalist), the play recently was named by Vietnam Vets of America, Inc.: "The most enduring play in the nation on Vietnam."

The Contest, received The Foundation for Jewish Culture Award, was directed by Jerry Zaks for Philadelphia's Annenberg Center, and originally premiered off-Broadway at The Ensemble Studio Theatre. In honor of its Applause publication, Phyllis Newman starred in the celebratory presentation of the play in New York. Samuel French published the acting edition in 2000.

Open Admissions, on Broadway, received one Tony Nomination, two Drama Desk nominations, a theatre World Award, a Samuel French Award, was a *New York Times* pick for "Ten Best Plays of the Year", and received the prestigious Dramatists Guild's Hull-Warriner Award. Ms. Lauro subsequently adapted the play for a CBS TV Special starring Jane Alexander and Estelle Parsons. In 2008 the play was honored by publication in *Writing Through Literature*, where it joined works by Walt Whitman, Ionesco, Langston Hughes and Toni Cade Bambera in the book's section, *"The Lesson"*.

Other work includes: *The Coal Diamond* (Heidemann Prize, Humana Festival; *"The Best Short Play Anthology"*; *NOTHING IMMEDIATE* (OOBA Festival Winner); *Railing It Uptown* (Playscripts, Inc., *"Take Ten Anthology;"*);

SUNDAY GO TO MEETIN' ("*30 Plays for Three Actors*", Humana Festival);
Pearls on the Moon (Ensemble Studio Theatre; Stamford Theatre Works with Joanna Merlin, Pauline Flanagan).

Ms. Lauro's novel, *The Edge* (Doubleday [Hardcover]; Dell[Softcover]): U.S.A., Weidenfeld & Nicolson(Hardcover) English Library(Softcover): Britain, was a Literary Guild Choice.)

Major Fellowships: The Guggenheim, 3 NEAs, The New York Foundation for the Arts. Affiliations: a Director of The Dramatists Guild Foundation, Board Member of League of Professional Theatre Women, Council Member of Ensemble Studio Theatre. Other affiliations: PEN, Writer's Guild East, Author's Guild, Playwrights/Directors Unit of The Actors Studio.

Also by
Shirley Lauro...

All Through the Night

Clarence Darrow's Last Trial

The Contest

I Don't Know Where You're Coming From at All!

Nothing Immediate

Open Admissions

A Piece of My Heart

OTHER TITLES AVAILABLE FROM SAMUEL FRENCH

CLARENCE DARROW'S LAST TRIAL

Shirley Lauro

Historical Drama / 4m, 4f

The story takes place in 1932, the last time Clarence Darrow pleads a major case in a criminal court of law. Set in various places in Chicago and Hawaii, Darrow, along with his wife, Ruby, travels to Honolulu to defend a Pearl Harbor Naval Lieutenant accused of shooting a Hawaiian who allegedly led a gang rape on the Lieutenant's wife.

**Winner! 2004 NEA "Access to Excellence Award",
in collaboration with New Theatre, Florida
Finalist! 2001 New American History Play Prize
Nominee! Carbonell 2006 Award, "Best New Play in Florida"**

"Shirley Lauro captures...the infamous Massie Case...
a compelling writer."
– *American Theater Magazine*

"The verdict on [Shirley Lauro's] latest play is that it can only add to her prizewinning ways."
– *The Entertainment News and Views*

"Interesting...with genuine emotion."
– *Miami Sun Sentinel*

Breinigsville, PA USA
15 April 2010
236182BV00002B/1/P